1973

To W. G. W.

COLLECTORS' BLUE BOOKS

Tiffany Glass

MARIO AMAYA

STUDIO VISTA, LONDON

FRONTISPIECE: Leaded glass doors, hollyhock design, ca. 1895, each panel 14 × 53 in. Courtesy Lillian Nassau, New York

Copyright © 1967 by Mario Amaya

Published in London by Studio Vista Ltd., Blue Star House, Highgate Hill, London N.19

SBN   289   37055   8

Printed in the United States of America
Designed by Joseph Bourke Del Valle

Acknowledgements

The author would like to thank the following people for their kind help and cooperation in collecting material and photographs for the book: Miss Mildred Constantine, Mr. Stuart P. Feld, Mr. Paul V. Gardner, Mr. F. Lanier Graham, Miss Anne Hochgraf, Mr. Charles Jerdein, Mr. J. Jonathon Joseph, Mr. Robert Koch, Mr. Hugh F. McKean, Mr. Hubert Rigg and Mr. J. Watson Webb, Jr.

Special thanks are due to Mr. James Coats who allowed the author to study his collection and provided many helpful ideas from the collector's point of view, and to Mrs. Lillian Nassau who gave generously much valuable time and advice. Most of all, much appreciation is due to Mrs. Joan Vass, without whose help this book could not have been possible, and to Mrs. Patricia White.

Hurricane lampshade (?) on patinated bronze stand, dull brown, patterned in threads of green to fawn shades, museum-dated ca. 1893–96, 14¼ in. high. The Metropolitan Museum of Art, Gift of H. O. Havemeyer, 1896

Tiffany Glass

DURING ITS HEYDAY, Art Nouveau produced more aesthetic exotica than perhaps any other style before it, but among the many extraordinary products it bred, Tiffany glass ranks the highest. Its quality and inventiveness apart, Tiffany Favrile glass was so much a part of the movement both in its conception and in its craft that its very name became synonymous with the style throughout America up to the outbreak of World War I.

Tiffany glass, with its swirling patterns, its strange, iridescent colors, its marbled designs, its curious free-form shapes, its clear, brilliant patternings trapped as if by magic in the texture of the object, was without a doubt the most beautiful glass produced in its time. In retrospect, it seems to take its place alongside some of the finest glass in history—from the Roman forms on which many of its pieces depend, to the Persian and Venetian prototypes from which it borrowed so much for inspiration. Moreover, it appears to an over-automated age that civilization may never again turn out such craftsmanship. Certainly Tiffany was the last great expression of an art form which itself has always indicated the level and progress of cultures. That this sophisticated handicraft could attain such a high watermark during an era when the decorative arts had reached a new low and at a time when machine-made "beauty" was for mass consumption, is not one of the least curious things about Tiffany.

To contemporary eyes Tiffany might seem a typical product of the "brown decades," a perfect example of the stylistic confusion that reigned—borrowing from here and there, mixing everything together in new combinations more for novelty and gimmickry than for meaningful design. In fact, it represented a remarkable breakthrough in design, and although it may have leaned heavily on oriental ornament and Near Eastern style, it is important to remember that at the time these trends indicated a refreshing departure from the slavish clichés of Renaissance and Louis Quinze.

It was Louis Comfort Tiffany who was responsible for all this—and his importance must also be measured by his influence on American taste generally at an early period in its development. At a time when U.S. millionaires were squandering mushroom fortunes on European arts and crafts—believing them to be the best that money could buy—Louis Comfort Tiffany broke new ground by convincing rich customers that *objets d'art* could be as beautifully made at home. He engendered confidence in his taste to such an extent that during the half century he was in business—from 1878 till the year before his death in 1933—the name Tiffany became a status symbol in design throughout the United States, and every well-furnished home possessed at least one hanging colored-glass lampshade, or one Favrile vase. As Larry Freeman in his study *Iridescent Glass* put it, "Overnight his iridescent glass became a thing of high fashion, and no home of wealth and refinement would be without it."

At a time when Tiffany's glass was astonishing his compatriots, America was, decoratively speaking, in a sorry state. The refined simplicities and functionalism of Henry Hobson Richardson had not made their impact felt as yet, and Edward Bok's *Ladies' Home Journal* was just beginning its battle for a simple, well-designed, average home. America was proving its talent for producing a number of world-changing inventions such as the telephone, the electric light, the typewriter, the gas engine, and an improved camera, but for aesthetic fare the country looked toward the latest European decorative fashions which were often totally unsuitable for a continent in the throes of a turbulent expansion and with a swelling middle class.

It was Tiffany's declared objective to forge a home-grown concept of restrained "beauty" based on the English Arts and Crafts movement, and on his countrymen's fervid search for an established cultural image. But with his *objets d'art*, mosaics, decorative stained-glass windows, electric lamps, furniture, fabrics, tapestries, jewelry, tiles, and above all his sumptuous Favrile glass, he also managed to equal, if not surpass, that continental luxury and richness so desired by the *nouveau-riche* American mercantile classes. In this there was an unconscious contradiction, but not to Tiffany. As he himself put it as late as 1917:

We are an extravagant people leading extravagant lives. It is the fashion to import from abroad furniture and decorations—but very few examples are consistent with our own civilization, ideals, mode of living, or for that matter, with a reasonable mode of life anywhere. But I must not rant against expenditure, which appears to be the fad. I would rather make a plea for a more restrained and reasonable decoration.

Good intentions aside, Tiffany glass must be seen as a decorative extravagance, more involved with style than with function or suitability; an unnecessary, albeit beautiful, adjunct to civilization. But then it was a time when Oscar Wilde could declare without any qualms: "All art is quite useless."

In his interiors, Tiffany was perhaps truer to ideals based on William Morris and sought to design things as a whole, not as a complex of individual parts; color schemes were harmonized, architectural details were unified, furniture was *en suite*, and everything was suitably simple. Tiles and glass were the decorative ornamental relief in what otherwise was a sensible, restrained atmosphere. We take this approach so much for granted today that it is difficult to see how Tiffany's interiors stood out against his contemporaries'. The taste of the times was a hodgepodge, as Lewis Mumford in his book *The Brown Decades* points out:

Beauty was defined in terms of visible possessions: no house was thought fit to live in that did not contain truckloads of ornament and bric-a-brac. With the steady growth of European travel among the richer classes, the acquisitive spirit throve; and presently the most fashionable architect, R. M. Hunt, was building French chateaux on Fifth Avenue, while less eminent rivals were designing Rhine castles for brewers or weird combinations of architectural souvenirs—an ecclecticism that reached its climax in a brilliant design, unfortunately not executed, for a building exhibiting a different historical style on every storey!

Tiffany's hands were not completely clean, but he went a long way toward clearing up the mess.

Louis Comfort Tiffany was born in 1848, the son of a man who was shortly to be America's smartest jeweler and silversmith. Charles Lewis Tiffany, who had founded Tiffany and Young in 1837, later called Tiffany, Young and Ellis, and still later Tiffany and Company, had dedicated himself to bringing to the doorsteps of the princes of industry the treasures they themselves had looked for abroad. By 1870, when Louis Comfort was twenty-two, the shop in its new Union Square premises in New York was the most famous jeweler's in the country. Millionaires could choose from the largest single collection of gems in the world, which included jewels which had once belonged to Marie Antoinette, the French Crown, and Prince Esterhazy. What is more, the elder Tiffany had set a new standard for American silver tableware, based on the English sterling standard, and his silver had won a prize at the Paris Exhibition in 1867, the first time an American silversmith had received an award from an international jury.

Tiffany's studio at the top of a building on 72 Street and Madison Avenue, New York, designed by himself with McKim, Mead and White, 1885. The house belonged to his parents. Reproduced courtesy of Mr. Robert Koch

With the Vanderbilts, the Astors, the Goulds, and the Havemeyers depending on Charles Tiffany to help them dispose of seemingly limitless fortunes, Louis Comfort must have grown up in a strange atmosphere of art and vulgarity, lavishness and restraint, aestheticism and rich extravagance. Underlying all the confusions, however, was his New England heritage which went back to a Squire Tiffany in 1660, and it was this to which he clung amid the onrush of mixed immigrant tastes from a variety of European backgrounds. His declared love of "good taste, true economy, and high standards of workmanship" can most likely be traced to a colonial past when such conditions were based on necessity, if not survival.

By the time Louis Comfort was eighteen and graduated from the Flushing Academy, Long Island, it was already certain that he was not grooming himself to take over the successful business his father had built in a brief quarter century. The Civil War had just ended and the Reconstruction boom had signaled a new era of expansion and wealth. There was little need to worry about security or the future. Tiffany decided he would be an artist rather than go to college, and he studied under the landscape painter George Inness, whose studio was a meeting place for young men who shared an interest in art. It was at Inness's studio that he met the playwright James Steele MacKaye, who in turn introduced him to Oscar Wilde years later when the Irishman came to lecture on "House Decoration." Indeed, Wilde's advice to Americans to bring together the artist and the handicraftsman on the one hand, and to introduce more color into interiors on the other, must have impressed Tiffany who sought throughout life to do both.

After a year of informal study with Inness (who was recognized as one of America's great landscape painters, notwithstanding his affinity to the French Barbizon school), Tiffany exhibited his first painting at the National Academy of Design. The following years (1868–69) he went to Paris to study with Leon Bailly who, along with Gérôme and other Salon artists, was much taken with the fashionable taste for North African and Near Eastern subjects and Islamic genre scenes. The Near Eastern styles that were to highlight Tiffany's decorative work in interiors and glass in the nineties and which were to be a minor motif of Art Nouveau, were probably first learned through this artist, just as his interest in Moorish decoration was doubtless first inspired by his trip to Spain during that time. It was there that he met another American artist, Samuel Colman, a pupil of Asher B. Durand, who had also gone abroad to study. In search of exotic subjects, they went to North Africa together where they executed watercolors and oils, and studied Islamic applied arts. Tiffany's paintings of this time indicate a clear grasp of form and a sensitive understanding of light and color. If he had stuck to painting, he most likely would have ranked among America's more interesting artists of genre and landscape.

But like so many others who were later to become the backbone and originators of Art Nouveau, fine art seemed too limiting. In fact, the division between fine and applied arts appeared arbitrary and meaningless in an age where the level of taste had fallen so low. If the painter or sculptor did not produce a beautiful pot or a well-designed textile, who else would? The Arts and Crafts movement which had been inspired in England by an alliance between William Morris and Edward Burne-Jones (with advice from Dante Gabriel Rossetti) in 1857 and was born indirectly out of the Pre-Raphaelite Brotherhood, seemed to point the moral way that art should go: fine art should be at one with the crafts and vice versa, and the division between the two should once and for all be banished; a renaissance of all the arts was needed and the Brethren dreamily looked back to the Middle Ages when every peasant had a home filled with "beautiful" things because they were fashioned by function and decorated with ornament that sprang not from other styles, but from abstractions of nature. By 1861, the firm of Morris, Marshall, Faulkner and Company, was a reality—later to become Morris and Company—existing as a direct inspiration for a more rational approach to design. With an output of fabrics, furniture, wall decorations, and stained glass, the name Morris became the *sine qua non* for the best in interior decoration and the applied arts. A host of other arts-and-crafts associations followed in its wake, throughout the eighties and nineties, but none achieved the international fame of Morris.

Another influence, never acknowledged, must have been Liberty and Company. The English branch of Tiffany and Company was opened in London at 221 Regent Street in 1868, the year Tiffany went to Europe to study painting. The Paris branch was opened in the same year. Although there is no evidence, it can be assumed the young scion of the jeweler visited the new premises, which was not far from Farmer and Rogers of Regent Street, a company that boasted an "Oriental Warehouse" run by the young Arthur Lazenby Liberty. Opened just after the 1862 exhibition in South Kensington, London, the Oriental Warehouse sold Japanese prints, drawings,

Gallery of H. O. Havemeyer house, Fifth Avenue at 66 Street, New York. Designed and decorated by the Tiffany Glass and Decorating Company, 1890–92. Note the hanging Tiffany lamps.

ABOVE: Cartoon for a window by Frank Brangwyn, 1899. Exhibited at the Grafton Galleries exhibition of Tiffany Glass, London, 1899. (whereabouts unknown)

OPPOSITE: *Autumn* from a window called *The Four Seasons*, 1890, 41 × 37⅝ in. Exhibited in Paris and London in 1892 and again in London in 1900. Collection, President Hugh F. McKean, Rollins College, Winter Park, Florida

lacquer, porcelain, bronzes, silks, fans and bric-a-brac. It was here that the American James McNeill Whistler, Rossetti, and others purchased their blue and white china and their Japanese prints which had become so fashionable among artists of the period in London and in Paris. Oriental art, which meant so much to Tiffany and which he was to collect later in life, might first have been brought to his attention in Regent Street. Another trip abroad was made by Tiffany in 1874–75, the year that Liberty decided to open his own shop at 218a Regent Street. The new firm attracted even more attention than the Oriental Warehouse, with customers such as Ruskin, Carlyle, Norman Shaw, Charles Keene, and of course artists such as Watts, Leighton, Millais and Alma-Tadema. If Tiffany missed the Oriental Warehouse on his first trip, it would have been impossible not to have heard of Liberty's on his second.

Moreover, it is not too farfetched to assume that a young, rich American in London with social connections—and particularly one interested in art—would have met the small circle that included Morris, Rossetti, Burne-Jones, not to mention his compatriot Whistler. Whistler was one of the most eager supporters of Japanese art which traveled westward after the 1859 treaty with Japan, and his transcription of oriental interior design into Western terms—clear color harmonies, light structural furniture, near-empty rooms, and almost bare walls—became one of the strongest influences on later Art Nouveau. In 1867, he had decorated his house with painted flowers and oriental motifs, gold leaf, flesh-colored walls, and blue and white china. When Tiffany began decorating houses in America in 1879, the one influence that shone strongest was Whistler, which makes it almost a foregone conclusion that he had firsthand knowledge of both Whistler's Peacock Room, done in London for Leland in 1877, and the Primrose Room, which Whistler sent to the 1878 Paris Exhibition, where Tiffany was exhibiting his own paintings.

Another important early source of Tiffany's interest in oriental art was Edward C. Moore, his father's chief designer who had worked with the firm since 1851, and under whose talents the company had won the gold medal at the Paris Exhibition of 1878. Moore was a heavy admirer of oriental *objets d'art*,

LEFT TO RIGHT: Flower-form vase, inscribed "L. C. Tiffany—Favrile v385," 11½ in. high. Miniature paperweight vase, inscribed "L. C. Tiffany—Favrile 8145D," 4 in. high. Paperweight vase with carved nasturtium blossoms, inscribed "L. C. Tiffany—Favrile 845A," 8¼ in. high. The J. Jonathon Joseph Collection, Boston

ABOVE: *La Cascade*, colored glass window by M. Besnard, executed by Tiffany. Exhibited at the Salon de Champs-de-Mars, 1895. Later installed in S. Bing's *La Maison de l'Art Nouveau*, Paris, December, 1895. (whereabouts unknown)

BELOW: *La Maternité*, colored glass window by Pierre Bonnard, executed by Tiffany. Exhibited at the Salon dê Champs-de-Mars, 1895. Later installed in S. Bing's *La Maison de l'Art Nouveau*, Paris, December 1895. (whereabouts unknown)

ABOVE: *Le Jardin*, colored glass window by K. X. Roussel, executed by Tiffany. Exhibited at the Salon de Champs-de-Mars, 1895. Later installed at S. Bing's *La Maison de l'Art Nouveau*, Paris, December, 1895. (whereabouts unknown)

BELOW: *St. Mark*, colored glass window, Episcopal Church, Islip, Long Island, 1878. The first example of a Tiffany window where the figuration is carried out by texture and color in the glass itself, without etching, staining or treating the surface of the glass.

ABOVE: Mosaic of Tiffany glass possibly made by Joseph Briggs, ca. 1900. Collection, Haworth Art Gallery, Accrington, England

BELOW: *La Moisson Fleurie*, colored glass window by Paul Ranson, executed by Tiffany. Exhibited at the Salon de Champs-de-Mars, 1895. Later installed in S. Bing's *La Maison de l'Art Nouveau*, Paris, December 1895. (whereabouts unknown)

and when he and Tiffany went to Paris they met Samuel Bing who had decided that Moore's designs, although oriental in inspiration, were in fact original designs in a "new style." Bing, whose shop, La Maison de l'Art Nouveau, actually gave the style its international name when it opened in 1895, sold oriental wares, in much the same way as Liberty in London. Seen in this light, it is not strange that the three great promoters of Art Nouveau, Tiffany of New York, Samuel Bing of Paris, and Liberty of London, all had an interest in oriental *objets d'art* and that all of them personally collected rare pieces.

Throughout this period, Tiffany exhibited his paintings frequently: at the Philadelphia Centennial in 1876, at the Paris Exhibition of 1878, and at the National Academy of Design, New York, the same year.

Married in 1872 to Mary Woodbridge Goddard, and already the father of two children, Tiffany began to expand his interests beyond the confines of painting, particularly after the Philadelphia Exhibition. Here he saw examples of Viollet le Duc's architecture (he had designed the Japanese section) and Walter Crane's wallpapers and designs which had won the Englishman a prize. Both men later provided source material for his own art.

The Philadelphia Centennial was instrumental in bringing together a group of people under the banner of the New York Society of Decorative Art. Candace Wheeler, who was its cornerstone, took up embroidery after studying the handiwork sent to the exhibition by the Kensington School of Art Needlework in England. It is interesting to note that another important creator of the Art Nouveau movement, Herman Obrist, was also involved in needlework and in fact began a school of embroidery in Florence. Soon Tiffany's student friend Samuel Colman was involved and he in turn convinced Tiffany of the Society's potential. Classes were organized exclusively for ladies "to encourage profitable industries among women," and art needlework, embroidery, and china and tile paintings were in the curriculum; Tiffany and Lockwood de Forest gave instruction in unbaked pottery. As models to follow, Mrs. Wheeler cited the designs of Morris, Burne-Jones, and "the direct and graceful work of Walter Crane, founded always upon forms of growth skillfully chosen. . . ."

But instructing gentlewomen in distress was not for Tiffany, and before a year was up, he had decided to go in for decorative work as a profession. "I believe there is more in it than painting pictures," he declared. At thirty-one, Tiffany formed a company with Samuel Colman and Candace Wheeler

LEFT: Opaque vase, part brown and green with oil colors worked together, part with striated surface imitating bronze, museum-dated ca. 1893–96, has original paper label: [Tif]fany Favrile Glass, and a second label with number printed in black "2169," 8⅝ in. high. The Metropolitan Museum of Art, Gift of H. O. Havemeyer, 1896

BELOW: Green and blue vase with peacock feather design, museum-dated ca. 1893–96, inscribed "01022," paper sticker with "TGD Co." (Monogram), 8⅛ in. high. The Metropolitan Museum of Art, Gift of H. O. Havemeyer, 1896

OPPOSITE: LEFT TO RIGHT: Iridescent vase, gold with flecks of brown, Tiffany Studios, inscribed "L.C.T. L712," 8 ⁹⁄₁₆ in. high. Reproduction of an antique glass vase, blue with greenish and purplish overtones and a nacreous finish, museum-dated 1912, inscribed "7239J L. C. Favrile," 5⅞ in. high. Flower-form vase, green stem rising to a peach-colored blossom, base of yellow and white striations, Tiffany Glass and Decorating Company, museum-dated 1898, inscribed "L. C. T. T1269," 18¹¹⁄₁₆ in. high. Gourd-shaped vase, wine colored with gold iridescence, Tiffany Glass and Decorating Company, museum-dated 1894–96, inscribed "56v," 7⅝ in. high. Elongated flower-form vase, base with yellow striations on white and yellow leaf pattern rising to a white blossom, Tiffany Glass and Decorating Company, inscribed "L. C. T. M247," 16¼ in. high. Paperweight bowl in ruby red with darker red patternings, Tiffany Studios, museum-dated 1903, inscribed "113A— Coll. L. C. Tiffany Favrile," 4½ in. high. The Metropolitan Museum of Art.

ABOVE: Morning-glory vase, flowers and leaves decorated in shades of blue and green, lower half translucent with slight gold luster, Tiffany Studios, museum-dated 1913, inscribed "150A—Coll. L. C. Tiffany—Favrile," 6⅝ in. high. The Metropolitan Museum of Art, Gift of the Louis Comfort Tiffany Foundation, 1951

BELOW: Gladioli vase, with an opalescent ground, Tiffany Studios, museum-dated 1909, inscribed "176A—Coll. L. C. Tiffany—Favrile," 16⅞6 in. high. The Metropolitan Museum of Art, Gift of the Louis Comfort Tiffany Foundation, 1951

ABOVE: Ten-sided agate vase with cut panels, marbleized design in green and yellow and spots of brown and tan along the ridges and at the top, Tiffany Studios, museum-dated 1905, inscribed "L. C. Tiffany—Favrile/Salon 1906/ 105—A Coll," 3 ¹³⁄₁₆ in. high. The Metropolitan Museum of Art, Gift of the Louis Comfort Tiffany Foundation, 1951

BELOW: Volcano (or lava) bowl, iridescent luster on outside, with shades of purple and blue in rough areas, inside iridescent blue and green, Tiffany Studios, museum-dated 1908, inscribed "21A— Coll. L. C. Tiffany—Favrile," 6⅝₁₆ in. high. The Metropolitan Museum of Art, Gift of the Louis Comfort Tiffany Foundation, 1951

Iridescent gold vase, museum-dated ca. 1893–96, inscribed "x2403," paper sticker with "TGD Co." (Monogram), 9⅛ in. high. The Metropolitan Museum of Art, Gift of H. O. Havemeyer, 1896

called Louis C. Tiffany and Associated Artists. Lockwood de Forest, who knew a great deal about East Indian handicrafts and fabrics, gave advice.

The Company, although known to few, began to gain publicity in art journals for its "harmonized" details, its high standards, and for its originality. One writer commended Tiffany's wallpapers for making a breach with old ideas and fashions, and for having an "unborrowed, individual look." Here were the seeds of Art Nouveau being sown.

The Associated Artists undertook a number of projects, remarkable for their variety. A drop curtain for the Madison Square Theatre (which subsequently was praised by Wilde when he visited America); the Fifth Avenue home of George Kemp; the Seventh Regiment Armory on Park Avenue (with Stanford White as consultant architect); the Union League Club on Fifth Avenue (in collaboration with John La Farge); and his own flat on the top floor of the Bella apartment house on East 26th Street. All these interiors were rich in oriental or Islamic detail, with exotic hanging lamps and lavish paneling, and they had one thing in common—Tiffany glass tiles as ornamental light relief and Tiffany colored glass windows.

Spurred on by the taste for medievalism, stained-glass windows were a popular form of decoration in the seventies. In England, William Morris and Company were producing them for churches and houses all over the country;

Burne-Jones was foremost among artists of this revived art form, first designing windows for James Powell and Sons, and later for Morris from 1861 till his death in 1898. Burne-Jones's windows were based on the traditional principles that went back at least to Chartres: the design allowed a number of small pieces of various colored glass to make up the broad figuration, with details, such as drapery folds, faces, feet, hands, etched into the glass with metallic oxides. After firing, the drawn design on the glass surface became part of the glass itself. The separate pieces of glass were joined together with "leading"— strips of grooved metal which outlined the design and held the structure of the window in place.

Stained-glass windows had gone into a decline since the Renaissance when fresco painting had taken over. Naturally more could be accomplished in terms of figurative illusionism with pigment on a flat plane than could be accomplished with thousands of bits of glass laboriously etched or stained, fired, and then threaded together with leading. By the nineteenth century, stained glass had been relegated to a picturesque craft as opposed to an art. But new industrial fortunes produced newer and bigger churches, and the demand for stained-glass windows multiplied. Some, like Burne-Jones's, were of high quality; others not so, among them the "Munich windows" manufactured for Americans in Germany. For a man of Tiffany's sensibilities and with his great knowledge of highly prized glass of the Eastern and Islamic countries, not to mention the great medieval stained-glass windows of France, to see such vulgar cheapened windows passing as a substitute for one of the most precious crafts ever invented by man, must have been irksome.

As early as 1875, he began to study the processes of medieval glassmaking and to experiment at the Thill Glasshouse, Brooklyn, with new methods of producing more varieties of color and texture. As he wrote later:

... I was confronted, amongst other problems, with the question what was to be done about windows since all window glass was of poor quality. I then perceived that the glass used for claret bottles and preserve jars was richer, finer and had a more beautiful quality in color than any glass I could buy. So I set to puzzling out this curious matter and found that the glass from which bottles are made contained the oxides of iron and other impurities which are left in the sand when melted.

The problem was how to make the metallic oxides left in the "impure" glass combine effectively, since the mix would disintegrate. It took thirty years of experimenting with new firing furnaces and new methods for annealing glass before he was entirely satisfied with the results.

The Associated Artists began to slip apart, with Candace Wheeler designing for commercial fabric houses, Lockwood de Forest traveling in the Far East and Samuel Colman living in Newport. After 1882 for a brief period the company was turned into Louis C. Tiffany and Company, with Associated Artists tagged on, and while it continued as America's foremost artistic decorating firm, it gave its founder more time to experiment with glass. As Candace Wheeler later recalled: "I think he was glad to get rid of us all for his wonderful experiments in glass iridescence." Tiffany worked at the Heidt Glasshouse in Brooklyn where the artist John La Farge was carrying out his own experiments in glass. La Farge did the painting and sculpture decorations for the Union League Club in 1881, while Tiffany provided the geometrically patterned colored glass windows, but there is no evidence as to who first became interested in a new type of glass. In 1881, both are credited with being foremost in new glass techniques and *Scribner's Monthly* reported:

[They] have virtually introduced a new industry of the most promising and interesting character. . . . The hot glass, while at a red heat, is rolled with corrugated rollers, punched and pressed by various roughened tools, or is squeezed and pressed up into corrugations by lateral pressure, or is stamped by dies. The "bull's-eyes" produced in making sheet glass, by whirling it round on a rod while still soft, are also cut into various shapes or, while still soft, are gently pressed into new shapes. . . . New styles of opalescent glass, new methods of mixing colors in the glasshouse, have also been tried, and with many surprising and beautiful results. Lastly comes one of the most original features of all, and this is the use of solid masses and lumps of glass pressed while hot into moulds, giving a great number of facets like a cut stone, or by taking blocks of glass and roughly chipping them into numerous small facets. These, when set in the window, have all the effects of the most brilliant gems, changing their shade of color with every changing angle of vision.

It can be assumed that the two men at the beginning worked closely together, exchanging ideas and discoveries. Later they became fierce competitors.

In 1896–97 when Europe, notably the Belgians and the French at Nancy were producing Tiffany type windows in large quantities, the *Magazine of Art* credited La Farge with being the originator: "John La Farge, after seeing in England certain painted windows from designs by Madox Brown, Rossetti and Burne-Jones, was the first American to contemplate the possibility of restoring colored glass to its ancient importance as an element in general decoration . . . Louis C. Tiffany, after him, went further on the scientific side . . . Thus, Mr. Louis C. Tiffany's glass had a double aim, he endeavored both to produce glass of equal quality with the early manufacture, as we see it softened by time, and to discover new methods, and produce new results such as might satisfy modern requirements, while faithful still to the old strict simplicity of style."

La Farge had begun experimenting in his Washington Square studio in 1876, blending premixed colors to produce an opalescent glass with various streaks of color and a milky texture. Tiffany had used mostly opalescent or translucent glass in abstract mosaic-type designs, and brightly colored opaque glass tiles, either marbled or iridized with colors ranging from reds, blues, greens to blacks, as wall decorations and fireplace surrounds up until this time. Some were of irregular shapes and thicknesses. He had used a "bull's-eye" semicircular window in the Church of the Sacred Heart, New York, in 1876 which looked like a series of tangential preserve-jar bottoms, crude but vigorous; moreover in 1878 his window for the Episcopal Church in Islip Long Island, with the subject of St. Mark, showed a similar series of tangential circular pieces of glass, surrounding the figure outlined in the broadest way, with delineations of face and hands kept to a minimum and no "drawing" on the glass to denote the draperies. The glass itself for the first time, by means of texture, changing color and form, was used as the sole means of describing light and shade and perspective. This was surely the breakthrough in colored glass windows that heralded the endless possibilities inherent in Tiffany's techniques.

Tiffany himself explained:

By the aid of studies in chemistry and through years of experiments, I have found means to avoid the use of paints, etching or burning, or otherwise treating the surface of the glass so that now it is possible to produce figures in glass of which even the fleshtones are not superficially treated—built up of what I call "genuine glass" because there are no tricks of the glassmaker needed to express flesh.

But if glass itself was to be the "draughtsman" (perhaps the first example in modern times of the medium being the message), if its own streaks, striations, imperfections, and colors were to "paint" the subject, then more varieties had to be found. Iridescence was one means of extending the color

ABOVE: Favrile covered jar in light green with applied feather motif, 19½ in. high. Illustrated as the frontispiece of a brochure "Tiffany Favrile Glass," 1896. Smithsonian Institution, Washington, D.C. (accessioned in 1896)

BELOW: Vase on bronze stand, marbleized in dull greens and browns with applied threaded and hooked decoration in yellowish white, ca. 1894, from The Tiffany Glass and Decorating Company, paper sticker with "TGD Co." (Monogram), and "Tiffany Favrile Glass, Registered Trademark," 8¼ in. high, on stand 10½ in. high. Smithsonian Institution, Washington, D.C. (accessioned in 1896)

ABOVE: Iridescent pale yellow-green Favrile glass vase with a darker foot, and applied decoration in pale gray-green leaf motif, ca. 1900, 5 in. high. Smithsonian Institution, Washington, D.C.

BELOW: Favrile blown glass vase, light amber body of bottle glass, with iridescent decorations of broad leaves in metallic blue, ca. 1894, from The Tiffany Glass and Decorating Company, paper sticker with "TGD Co." (Monogram), and "Tiffany Favrile Glass, Registered Trademark," 6 in. high. Smithsonian Institution, Washington, D.C. (accessioned in 1896)

LEFT: Marbleized Favrile glass vase, decoration on dull green, amber and dark brown, with black matt leaf form, ca. 1894, from The Tiffany Glass and Decorating Company, paper sticker with "TGD Co." (Monogram), and "Tiffany Favrile Glass, Registered Trademark," 5 in. high. Smithsonian Institution, Washington, D.C. (accessioned in 1896)

RIGHT: Favrile green vase of bottle glass, with applied fish decoration in colors, wave motif and outlines of fish engraved on the surface by lapidary's wheel, ca. 1896, 7⅛ in. high. Smithsonian Institution, Washington, D.C. (accessioned in 1896)

OPPOSITE: Iridescent gold decanter with stopper, ca. 1900, signed on base "L. C. Tiffany," 10 in. high. Smithsonian Institution, Washington, D.C., Gift of the Aaron & Lillie Straus Foundation, Inc.

range of glass and Tiffany used the example of buried Roman and Persian glass to see if he could equal it in texture and color.

Iridescence was not new when Tiffany began his experiments. Iridescent glass, which eventually became almost as much a trademark of Art Nouveau as the whiplash curve, came into being probably at mid-century with a craze for antique glass dug up at Pompeii and Rome. In 1873, Ludwig Lobmeyer showed the first commercially produced iridescent glass. He was followed by Count Harrach of Neuwelt, Bohemia. The English firm of Thomas Webb and Sons along with three other companies were making this kind of glass in 1878. Lobmeyer exhibited his glass that year in Paris at the exhibition in which Tiffany was showing his paintings. In 1879, C. F. A. Hinricks of New York was selling iridescent Bohemian glass and "bronze" glass. Meanwhile Webb had displayed at the Paris Exhibition of 1878 and at the newly opened Grosvenor Gallery in London, a new iridescent "bronze" glass in shapes which were advertised as having been "borrowed from Dr. Schliemann's finds at Troy and Mycenae." Such glass, seen at the same gallery in which Alma-Tadema's evocations of the everyday antique world had helped to launch a new interest in Roman civilization, made a deep impression on the public and was an immediate commercial success.

The popularity of iridescent glass at this time is indicated by the facts unearthed by A. C. Revi in his book *19th Century Glass*: in March, 1877, Louis Clemandot registered a patent in Paris; five months later Thomas Webb in London laid claim to the same technique whereby hot glass was subjected to metallic chloride fumes which produced a bluish-purple glass with highlights of coppery red and gold (Thomas Goode and Sons of London sold Webb's "bronze" glass); in November of the same year Sidney Witmann of London was given protection for a system of iridizing glass by boiling it in muriatic acid under intense pressure; in 1878, Mount Washington Glass in the United States patented an iridescent or "rainbow" process using carbonic acid fumes; in 1881, McDermott of Surrey patented an iridescent process as did Rice W. Harris at Calais; in 1889, Franz Emile Grosse of Berlin patented an effect produced by using fumes from "pink salts" and in 1892, John Jacobson of Boston registered a method in England.

When Tiffany filed for a patent in 1880 for making a decorative iridescent glass which he was later to call *Favrile* after the old English word *fabrile* meaning "made by hand," he was by no means the first. What is more, his technique at that time was not unique as is clearly stated in his patent claim for "new and useful Improvements" which . . .

. . . consist in a metallic luster, changeable from one to the other, depending upon the direction of the visual ray and the brilliancy or dullness of the light falling upon or passing through the glass. . . . The metallic luster is produced by forming a film of a metal or its oxide, or a compound of a metal, on or in the glass either by exposing it to vapors or gasses or by direct application. It may also be produced by corroding the surface of the glass, such processes being well known to glass manufacturers.

Thus, all the tales about secret alchemy, accidental discoveries, lost recipes recovered from ancient manuscripts, which have always surrounded Tiffany glass, hold no water.

With continuous experimentation that produced an ever-increasing range of textures and colors, Tiffany glass and mosaic tiles became the most-sought-after form of applied decoration, used by most fashionable architects, Stanford White among them. It is difficult to distinguish a Tiffany-designed window from one designed by a competitor or a colleague using his glass if the window in question does not appear on any of the three lists of windows compiled by Tiffany's firm*; the distinction must be based on careful scrutiny of details of the window itself. Many windows designed by others were either manufactured by him or incorporated his glass. Windows from his studios which contain the patented iridescent glass are all either by him or from his workshop. Many Tiffany windows before 1890 are geometrically or abstractly designed with little or no figuration. These are considered by some "modernists" his best works, but his figurative windows tested his resources more completely.

Robert Koch in his study of Tiffany, *Rebel in Glass*, points out that windows made before 1892 are marked *Tiffany Glass Co.* Those produced between 1892 and 1900 usually bear the inscription *Tiffany Glass & Decorating Co.* After 1900 they are marked either *Tiffany Studios* or *Louis C. Tiffany.* He states that windows made for private customers are difficult to identify since they might have no markings or might have lost their markings which usually appear in the

---

*The first list of 1893 recorded some of the churches and public buildings in twenty-four states and Washington, D.C., where Tiffany's work could be found. The second list, a detailed one of 95 pages, was published as a pamphlet in 1897 and is at the Avery Architectural Library of Columbia University. The third one, *A Partial List of Windows,* appeared in 1915 and a copy is at the Boston Public Library.

lower right-hand corner. Again, only external comparisons with other known windows and a close investigation of the general design and the way the glass is set and used, can offer proof.

"Tiffany-type" windows sprouted over all America, in the homes of the *nouveau-riche* from Seattle to San Francisco, in churches from New England to the Middle West. Bowery saloons, smart flats, suburban houses, even the elevated railway waiting-rooms were covered with colored glass windows, most of them a cheapened variety of the Tiffany sort. But to have a house actually decorated by Tiffany himself was the true mark of sophistication. What is more, Tiffany had all the means and wealth at his disposal for installing luxurious "artistic" accessories tastefully. He also cleverly kept his eye turned toward the latest exotic fashions in interiors whether inspired by Byzantine decor, Islamic art or by Whistler. Tiffany was called upon to decorate interiors for J. Taylor Johnston, founder of the Metropolitan Museum of Art; Hamilton Fish; and Mark Twain. Cornelius Vanderbilt II eagerly approved Tiffany's plans to decorate his new mansion, and Ogden Goelet's "showplace residence" came in for the Tiffany treatment. James Gordon Bennett's yacht *Namouna* was also on the list, and the firm decorated James Steele MacKaye's new Lyceum Theatre for a fee of $50,000 which was never recovered since the theatre failed in its first season. No matter about the cost, it was considered the country's first "aesthetic" theatre. It was also the first theatre to use electricity throughout and Tiffany worked with Thomas Alva Edison in designing the chandeliers and wall lights which were described as "soft, pleasant, diffused."

But Tiffany reached the apogee of success when President Arthur asked him to decorate the White House. With a shrewd understanding of the value of publicity which was to promote his thriving business throughout his career, Tiffany advertised completion of redecorating the State Dining Room, the East Room, the Red Room, and the Blue Room in 1883, in a remarkably short time at a remarkably low cost of about $30,000. Ceilings were bronzed or silvered, Sienna Axminster carpets were ordered by the yard, new curtains run up, furniture recovered, mosaic tile fireplaces installed, gaslit sconces made to order in the form of rosettes three feet wide incorporating the newly patented Favrile iridescent glass and mosaic. These extraordinary sounding sconces were ornamented with iridescent glass pendants and decorated with silvered lead.

The major single job in the White House was replacing the ground-glass hall screen that divided the corridor from the drafty vestibule. A gigantic screen of opalescent glass, in brightly colored panels featuring national emblems, demonstrated one of the earliest uses of the swelling and receding "organic" free forms, encased in geometric leading, which became so popular in high Art Nouveau a decade later.

If the White House was Tiffany's most prestigious job, the Havemeyer's Fifth Avenue residence in New York in 1890–92 earned him back the reputation he was losing among fellow decorators and artists who thought him too commercial. The Havemeyer residence could never be called "commercial." In fact, it was a flight of fantasy installed with skill and restraint, presenting a series of linked interiors which had a unified appearance and—despite their lavishness—a simplified, uncluttered disposition. The Havemeyers were at the time the most enlightened collectors of both modern and traditional art, and the house was to be a repository for a truly great assembly of paintings, including works by Manet, Rembrandt and El Greco. The hall was covered entirely in white mosaic patterns, inspired partly by Byzantine mosaics in the church at Ravenna. The staircase was thought to have been derived from the one at the Doge's palace in Venice; the music room walls were hung with Chinese embroideries and covered with Chinese carpets; the furniture, composed of thin, vertical carved struts, was rubbed with gold leaf and varnished to look like Japanese ivory *inro*. The *pièce de résistance* was the hanging golden staircase which was suspended around an open balcony in the picture gallery. With the treads supported by one piece of curving cast iron, the handrailing and ballustrades, which dangled magically, were gold filigree interspersed with dozens of small crystal balls. The decor included hanging electric lamps of two types: heavy bulbous Eastern forms with swirling interlaced patterns filled in with pieces of iridescent glass; and fragile chandeliers hung on thin chains and terminating in spreading branches which held light clusters of "buds" or "pods" of small iridescent globes that floated upward. Mrs. Havemeyer was delighted, and Samuel Bing, when he came to New York, was so overwhelmed that he flatly declared, "*Nothing* could achieve such a unified concept in an interior." Certainly the simplified structural design throughout, notwithstanding the enormous collection of pictures and oriental *objets d'art* that had to be accommodated, was a new theme which perhaps only Arthur Heygate Mackmurdo in England had achieved up to that time and one which was to influence most English Art Nouveau architects from Voysey to Charles Rennie Mackintosh.

In 1885, Tiffany had proved himself an architect of some originality by designing with McKim, Mead and White a house for his family on Madison Avenue and 72nd Street which was based on Richardson's Romanesque style of architecture and which contained a top floor studio for his use. In a series of articles in 1897–98 in the magazine *Studio*, Cecilia Waern noted that his studio was "still more eclectic, as the whole street front of a house in India has been taken and combined with a truly gorgeous American window, with lamps, chains, plants of many lands, in a kind of decorative jungle." In the middle of the "jungle" was a remarkable free-form central fireplace with gentle "organic" curves reaching upward in a single column toward the roof, like "the bole of a great tree." The fireplace was open on four sides, so that its blazing logs would illuminate the iridescent lamps and the bright vases, bowls, and plaques which were everywhere. As described by Charles de Kay in *The Art Work of Louis C. Tiffany* (published privately by Tiffany in 1914), "Colored tiles and the cinnabar red so much loved by the Japanese, iridescent glass and shelves full of ceramics in subdued tones meet the eye in every direction."

In 1885, with the commercial success of his firm soundly reestablished after the loss of money over the Lyceum Theatre failure, Tiffany renamed the business the Tiffany Glass Company. Set up in a more business-like manner, it catered to professional decorators, designers, and architects rather than to private individuals. The decorating side of the business receded into the background apart from special commissions such as the Havemeyer residence or the Pratt Institute Library in Brooklyn (1896). The glass, which had proved such an overwhelming success and which was being copied everywhere, took up most of his attention.

He had set up his own furnaces in 1880 with the help of a Venetian glass-blower, Andrea Boldini, who came from the Salviati factory in Murano. But after two disastrous fires he continued to work at the Heidt Glasshouse, Brooklyn, until 1893. Boldini's importance to Tiffany is difficult to determine; suffice it to say that through the Italian the entire knowledge of Venetian glassblowing and throwing was at the disposal of the American. What is more, some early Tiffany vases bear a striking resemblance in color and texture to the mid-nineteenth-century glass at the Murano Museum, Venice.

LEFT: Favrile vase formed as a Persian perfume-sprinkler, smoky green iridescent, with conventionalized plant forms in red and veined in various colors, and white, unsigned, torn off label, "+1279" scratched on base, 16 in. high. Purchased at Tiffany and Company, Regent Street, 1896. Victoria and Albert Museum, London

RIGHT: Red vase with orange tinges and silvery blue flower leaves and long stems, museum-dated 1898–99, signed "L. C. T." with label of Tiffany Glass and Decorating Company, as well as a second label marked "Zoll 1130," 5½ in. high. Victoria and Albert Museum, London

OPPOSITE RIGHT: Brown, iridescent Favrile vase with blue, green and gold vertical leaf-shaped devices, unsigned, paper sticker with "TGD Co." (Monogram), numbered " + 1457," label "Zoll 1130," also stock number label, 15½ in. high. Purchased at Tiffany and Company, Regent Street, 1896. Victoria and Albert Museum, London

OPPOSITE LEFT: Base detail of vase at the right.

OPPOSITE BELOW: Paper sticker (Monogram) on Tiffany glass pieces accessioned by the Smithsonian Institution in 1896.

ABOVE: Marbleized bottle vase, transparent mahogany-colored glass marbled in red, green, blue and brown, Tiffany Glass and Decorating Company, museum-dated ca. 1893–94, labeled "[Ti]ffany Fabrile Glas[s]." Possibly by Arthur Nash. 5⅝ in. high. The Metropolitan Museum of Art, Gift of H. O. Havemeyer, 1896

BELOW: Detail of the above showing label and stock number.

On a trip to Paris in 1889 for the *Exposition Universelle*, Tiffany was shocked to see that a window by his competitor John La Farge was the center of attraction and was winning widespread praise for its unique coloring and texture. He had produced much better examples of such windows. Since Edward Moore was also in Paris to receive the Chevalier of the National Legion of Honor and to collect the Grand Prix and five gold medals for his work for Tiffany and Company, the solution was clear. Tiffany would make windows for Moore's friend Bing which would far outshine anything anyone else was producing. Still trading mostly in oriental wares and Eastern *objets d'art*, Bing had become a focal point of the new movements in art that were fulminating in Paris at that time. Many fine artists, thoroughly dismayed by what they saw around them, were turning to the applied arts, and foremost among them—no doubt prodded and pushed by Bing—were the Nabis, a small group of painters inspired by Emile Bernard and Gauguin and the new Pont-Aven school. The separation of color into pure, flat planes as it was so well achieved in medieval stained-glass windows, fascinated the Nabis and they attempted to work out their pictures through a system called *Cloisonnisme* which broke down forms and colors into delineated compartments, like cloisonné enamel-work. Through this technique they hoped to achieve a *Synthesisme*, as it was called, between subject, materials and picture plane which would coalesce into a unified whole.

What Tiffany had been doing in America came very close to the Nabis. Although in 1889 they were not yet a movement, and many of them were still studying at the Académie Julian, by August, 1890, Maurice Denis had published their theories in an article entitled *Art et Critique* aligning their work to the decorative arts. He reflected the view of their mentor Gauguin who had boldly declared "all art is decoration." The Dutch Nabi, Verkade, later described that decisive moment:

In the early part of 1890 the war cry went out from studio to studio: "No more easel pictures! Away with useless bits of furniture! Painting must not usurp a freedom which cuts it off from other arts! The painter's work begins where the architect decides his work is finished! Give us walls, and more walls to decorate! Down with perspective! The wall must be kept as a surface and must not be pierced by representation of distant horizons. There are no such things as pictures, only decoration."

This surely was what Tiffany as a painter-cum-craftsman had been striving toward for nearly a decade, and his reunion with Bing, whom he had first known of in 1879, was the impetus that his work needed if it was to move decisively into the twentieth century.

The first product of their association, which was to be a long and advantageous one, was a window called "The Four Seasons." Bearing the date "Anno Domini MDCCCC," it was exhibited in Paris in 1892, and later in London. It was the first work by Tiffany in what could be called high Art Nouveau, years before the style reached maturity throughout Europe. A "domestic window" ostensibly made for the home of Walter Jennings, its descriptive panels of the four seasons enclosed in cartouches were overwhelmed by an ornamental border of *entrelac* designs reminiscent of Celtic illuminations. The interlaced patterns wound their way around the rectangular window to find themselves enmeshed in a stylized eagle at the top and a row of five vases at the bottom, conceived in the most generalized terms. The four "abstracted" paintings of the seasons symbolically evoked the times of the year with colorful vegetation and landscape, and were edged by free-flowing decorative borders with jewel-like insets of colored glass recalling those of a Byzantine reliquary. "Summer" is perhaps the most evocative of these four panels; overhung with leafy shapes, its heavy-leaded outlines describe grassy hillocks and outsize roses, a distant lake and purplish mountains beyond. Perspective and form are indicated by the striations and changing colors in the glass itself and there is no etching or staining on the material.

One can only speculate on the question of influence here—of how much Tiffany influenced, or was influenced by, the Nabis, among them Maurice Denis, Vuillard, Bonnard, Ibels, Ranson, and Roussel. However, a system of creating imagery out of separated areas of flat color chosen arbitrarily for its decorative effect rather than for its truth to nature, had been developed by Tiffany for over a decade before he came into contact with the Nabis. Moreover, the example of Sérusier's "Talisman," painted at Pont-Aven with Gauguin's help and brought back to Paris in 1888, by itself was hardly enough to lead the Nabis into their later work which consciously attempted in paint to parallel the visual effect of stained glass, cloisonné enamelwork, and even Byzantine mosaics. A master of stained glass, on the other hand, could teach them more about the methods of color separation and linear design than any talisman.

LEFT TO RIGHT: Paperweight vase with purple convolvulae and green leaves, the interior with iridescence, inscribed "L. C. Tiffany—Favrile. Panama-Pacific Ex. 2392J," 6¼ in. high. Flower-form vase with pale yellow horizontal waves and trailings, super-imposed with reddish brown upright leafage, the foot shaded from amber at the center to green at the rim, 11¾ in. high. Paperweight vase, invested over the red glass with a collar of trailing ochre and green vine-like motifs on a shaded turquoise blue and green ground, inscribed "L. C. Tiffany 27A-Coll," 8⅞ in. high. Formerly, Coats-Connelly Collection

Bing went to America to make a survey of art and architecture for the French Government and while in New York saw a great deal of Tiffany. Together they discussed the decorative arts of the future and came to the conclusion that everything depended not only, as Morris had suggested, on keeping the handicrafts alive, but also on new machines which could produce beauty in the home for a wider public. How this was to be achieved without lowering standards of craftsmanship could not be quite foreseen. Meanwhile, the taste of the rich bourgeoisie must be raised to a new level of refinement. It was Bing who prompted Tiffany to design a chapel for the World's Columbian Exhibition in Chicago in 1892, which would make use of iridescent and stained glass, mosaics, tiles, and metalwork, in fact every aspect of Tiffany's art which he had been developing for over ten years. The chapel, which was not ready for the opening, arrived in Chicago in 1893 after first being exhibited in New York. It immediately became the sensation of the exhibition.

Designed in a neo-Byzantine style which recalled earlier works by Richardson, and reflecting directly the idiom that Louis Sullivan at that moment was making popular, the chapel with its "dark" and "light" room contained all the richness and lavishness of Constantinople. And yet, because all the luxurious detailing was an integral part of the overall architectural design, the chapel had a spacious air of simplicity and modernity about it; every element was part of a unified whole, fused into a comprehensive pattern that took into account the complex surface ornament. The white marble altar had a white and iridescent glass mosaic front, and the reredos was made of iridescent blue and green mosaics in the forms of peacocks and scrolls, set in black marble. The entire altar was held together by a series of Romanesque arches, supported by groups of columns covered over completely with glass mosaics in red, green, and brown in abstract patterning. This sort of modernized Byzantine/Romanesque apse was finished in a million pieces of flashing glass and marble mosaic, relieved with pearls and semiprecious stones. The peacock reredos, surrounded by a wide expanse of glistening, opalescent surfaces that sparkled in the reflected light of a great hanging chandelier made of hundreds of iridescent glass balls, was considered a splendid coda to the Capella Palatina at Ravenna. Flanking it, the "dark" room was in colors ranging from pale yellow-greens to dark blue-greens in a subtly shifting spectrum, and the "light" room was in silver and opal, lit by a chandelier of mother-of-pearl. The entire effect had at once a luxurious atmosphere and a striking simplicity for which Tiffany was famous. Visitors overlooked allusions to earlier styles and considered the chapel to be one of the most "modern" works on show.

Romanesque arches were popular that year and Louis Sullivan, who had known Tiffany's work at first hand in the eighties, had also produced a series of concentric Romanesque arches for the Transportation Building entrance. The "Golden Door," as it was known, won three medals.

Mosaics had interested Tiffany as far back as 1880 when he experimented with a new variety of colors, but it was not until 1889 that he began to use them extensively, first in churches, and then, most notably, in the Havemeyer residence. His technique was different from others' and he incorporated his patented iridescent glass combined, with transparent pieces backed with gold or metal leaf. As it was described: "Pieces of glass were selected, cut out and assembled upon the working drawing, then reassembled, face downward, upon a table and covered with cement mortar to form a slab with the glass embedded in its surface, the mortar backing, being white, reflected the light through the glass in a softly luminous effect." He designed several mosaic figure works which are more noteworthy for their brilliant color effects than for their style or composition. His most ambitious project in mosaic was the pulpit made in 1895–97 of inlaid marble and glass mosaic for St. Michael's Church, New York, which was almost an exact copy of a Romanesque proto-type.

By 1895, Bing had already finalized plans to turn his shop into a showcase for the newest in applied and fine arts: under the name of La Maison de l'Art Nouveau, the premises at 22 rue du Province opening in December of that year would become an adventurous example of what could and should be achieved in furniture, tapestries, fabrics, wallpapers, metalwork, glass, and *objets d'art*. Nothing was to depend directly on styles of the past; everything was to be conceived in terms of the *new*—a dramatic break from tradition which would lead the age out of the labyrinth of ornamental confusion into the clear light of a new century. Although Bing and Tiffany both prized craftsmanship above all else, Bing eagerly accepted into his shop machine-made objects such as brass and copper lamps by Benson of England, so long as such objects proved to be of aesthetic merit. The interiors were designed by Bonnier, and the exterior painted by Frank Brangwyn. Tiffany was called upon to provide a dazzling set of colored glass windows which were designed by the Nabis and their fellow travelers.

Exhibited at the Salon du Champs-de-Mars before being installed in Bing's shop, the windows caused much controversial comment and many critics thought them ridiculous just because they didn't rely on the traditional methods of staining and etching designs into the glass. The *Revue des Arts Decoratifs* noted that Tiffany was exhibiting "a dozen windows, *transcriptions in American glass of a series of compositions by French artists of an independent group.*" The artists listed were M. Bernard ("La Cascade"), Paul Ranson ("La Moisson Fleurie"), K. X. Roussel ("Le Jardin"), Pierre Bonnard ("La Maternité"), P.-A. Isaac ("Iris et Roseaux"), G. H. Ibels ("L'été"), Vuillard ("Les Marronniers"), Maurice Denis ("Une Paysage"), Toulouse-Lautrec ("Papa Chrysanthème"), and Félix Vallotton ("Une Parisienne").

When the windows were exhibited in the shop in December, 1895, the artists participating were listed as Vuillard, Bonnard, Toulouse-Lautrec, Ibels, Sérusier, Grasset, Vallotton, Roussel and Ranson (who designed two); ten windows in all.

The following year, the *Magazine of Art* remarked that Ranson's window was "a typical instance" of Tiffany glass with "fragments of various natural materials, transparent slices of pebbles or precious crystals. These split, cut, and polished, give singular beauty to his [Tiffany's] work, with effects undreamed of by our forefathers."

This set of windows, whose whereabouts is unfortunately unknown, stands as one of the great statements of Art Nouveau which could combine so effectively the fine and the applied arts. As depicted in photographs, the window by Bonnard appears the most beautiful, with mother and child in an *intimiste* pose, depicted in the most summary black leaded outlines, filled in with marbled, striated opalescent and iridescent glass which builds up the color, form, and perspective of the scene. When the windows were shown three years later at the Salon de Champs de Mars, Bing extravagantly claimed Tiffany glass was superior even to medieval glass. In 1899, Tiffany executed a number of windows to Frank Brangwyn designs which from all accounts were equally striking, although the cartoons did not have the tense, linear rhythm of the Nabi windows nor their structural disposition.

While his colored glass windows were setting the fashion, Tiffany had long since embarked on a new experiment: Favrile glass *objets d'art*. Setting up his own glasshouse once more in 1893 in Corona, Long Island, this time he called on the advice of an Englishman Arthur Nash. In 1882, Nash of Stourbridge,

ABOVE: Pinch bottle vase with silver and blue iridescent swirls, having a stone-like texture, inscribed "L.C.T. R1827," with label, 4 in. high. Formerly, Coats-Connelly Collection

BELOW: Miniature vase, deep blue with iridescent upright leaf fronds, inscribed "Louis C. Tiffany, 03242," 2¾ in. high. Formerly, Coats-Connelly Collection

ABOVE: Clear green and white paper-weight vase, with daisies above trailing green leaves and vines, inscribed "L.C. Tiffany-Favrile, 2904G," 5 in. high. Formerly, Coats-Connelly Collection

LEFT: Paperweight vase, amber, with mauve blossoms and deep green leaves with trailing vines, superimposed by pale blue and green horizontal swirls, blown aperture at base, inscribed "L.C.T. Y5617," 4 in. high. Formerly, Coats-Connelly Collection

RIGHT: Purple and brown pyriform vase, with three upright swirled forms in tones of purple and turquoise on a deep brown ground, inscribed "Louis C. Tiffany Favrile, 359J," 4¼ in. high. Formerly, Coats-Connelly Collection

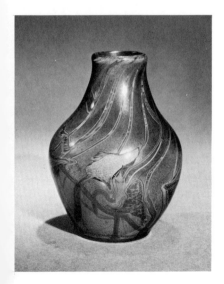

one of the employees of Thomas Webb of Stourbridge, a firm that had been making iridescent glass since 1878, took out a patent for "vasa Murrhina," a type of spangle or splatterdash glass with a transparent body which was embedded with flakes of mica. Nash, from most accounts, was asked to superintend the building of the factory for Tiffany and doubtless played an integral part in the development of Tiffany glass from this moment on. His influence on the type of Favrile glass that was produced in the next fifteen years cannot be overestimated, since he brought with him all the methods of one of the leading British pioneers of modern glass as well as traditional English types. Nash ran the factory with his two sons, A. Douglas and Leslie, and later the Nashes claimed much credit for the new varieties of glass that Tiffany produced. They even went so far as to say they were "responsible for all the designs, glass formulae and decorating techniques" although this was never acknowledged by Tiffany himself.

Reorganizing the company in 1894 as the Tiffany Glass and Decorating Company, in Jersey City and New York City, Tiffany obviously was eager to infiltrate into every household in America objects which were either useful or merely decorative for he firmly believed, as he wrote in an article entitled "The Gospel of Good Taste," "It is all a matter of education, and we shall never have good art in our homes until people learn to distinguish the beautiful from the ugly. . . ." In beginning with vases and glass ornamental ware, Tiffany may have had in mind the example of Emile Gallé of Nancy, whose glass vases and *objets d'art* he had seen at the Paris Exhibition of 1889. But Gallé's glass was firmly linked to traditional types at this time and depended heavily on oriental examples; he used enameling, etching, cameo decoration, complicated overlay work and groundings. Tiffany was determined that the glass itself should be the decoration, and hoped to produce pieces that were formed naturally out of their own material with a minimum of applied hand-decoration. As in his windows, the material itself had to do the work.

LEFT TO RIGHT: Paperweight vase with frieze of elongated undersea forms interspersed with starfish, inscribed "L. C. Tiffany—Favrile, 4A—Coll," 4¼ in. high. Vase decorated with scrolled lappets, inscribed "L. C. Tiffany—Favrile, 199A—Coll," 4½ in. high. Faceted agate vase, lower half marbleized, inscribed "L. C. Tiffany—Favrile, 104A-Coll," 3¼ in. high. Clear paperweight vase decorated with convolvulae and leaves, inscribed "L. C. Tiffany, 1362J," 6¼ in. high. Paperweight vase, inscribed "L. C. T., Y5402," 7¾ in. high. Formerly, Coats-Connelly Collection

ABOVE: Black iridescent vase with carved ochre and blue leaves, inscribed "L. C. Tiffany—Favrile 102A-Coll," 3½ in. high. The J. Jonathon Joseph Collection, Boston

OPPOSITE: LEFT TO RIGHT: Blue iridescent flower-form Favrile vase, inscribed "85 H.L.C. Tiffany Favrile," 20½ in. high. Opaque amber glass decorated with sienna leaves and vines between layers of clear glass, inscribed "9163C L. C. Tiffany Favrile," also has paper label, 6⅜ in. high. Transparent pale yellow Favrile flower-form vase with white striations in brown leaf forms, inscribed "L. C. T." and "07653," 11⅜ in. high. Collection, The Museum of Modern Art

Nash, who was known as "a wizard with a blowpipe," most likely produced the earliest flower-form vases—glass objects in free-flowing shapes which sprouted from circular bases and surged upward on fragile stems, flowering out into globes, the striations and swirls of color in the glass following the shape as it ascended from bottom to top. Nash is said to have been able to blow an ordinary piece of bottle glass and then by applying various rods of colored glass fused to the surface, make the object take on the shape of the coloring that had been let in. Out of this technique came those sensuous "organic" natural forms so closely associated with Art Nouveau. It was presumably Arthur Nash who invented the "peacock" iridescent vases with striations in the glass resembling the markings of a peacock feather; that the peacock motif should be incorporated was a foregone conclusion. After all, Whistler had made the satiny green-blue iridescent peacock colorings one of the hallmarks of the style.

Naturally the first experiments in glass *objets d'art* were sent to Bing for the opening of his Maison de l'Art Nouveau. Bing could not believe the results, registering amazement that "after all the accomplishments of the Venetians, of Gallé and others, it was still possible to innovate, to utilize glass in a new way that was often opaque and matt, with a surface that was like skin to the touch, silky and delicate." The method itself was described in some detail by Bing:

Look at the incandescent ball of glass as it comes out of the furnace; it is slightly dilated by the initial inspiration of air. The workman charges it at certain pre-arranged points with small quantities of glass, of different textures and different colours, and in the operation is hidden the germ of the intended ornamentation. The little ball is then returned to the fire to be heated. Again it is subjected to a similar treatment (the process sometimes being repeated as many as twenty times), and, when all the different glasses have been combined and manipulated in different ways, and the article has been brought to its definite state as to form and dimensions, it presents this appearance: the *motifs* introduced into the ball when it was small have grown with the vase itself, but in differing proportions; they have lengthened and broadened, while each tiny ornament fills the place assigned to it in advance in the mind of the artist.

Thus all sorts of internal ornamentation could be fused into the glass: flower decorations in the form of gladioli, morning glories, irises, roses, trailing leaves and stems, or just colored abstractions known as "Accidentals." In

ABOVE: Clear paperweight vase, with a pattern of trailing vines and yellow and green leaves, inscribed "L.C. Tiffany—Favrile, 7967J," 6 in. high. Formerly, Coats-Connelly Collection

BELOW: Blue paperweight vase with a trellis of large formalized blossoms, ochre leaves and vertical vines, silver iridescent interior, and a pierced base, inscribed "L. C. Tiffany—Favrile, 8156D," 8¾ in. high. Formerly, Coats-Connelly Collection

LEFT TO RIGHT: Dimpled vase in clear yellow iridescent glass with yellowish-green and pale purple striations, unsigned, paper sticker with "TGD Co." (Monogram), label marked "Zoll 1130 4871," 6¾ in. high. Purchased at Tiffany and Company, Regent Street, 1896. Green Favrile vase, with iridescent leaf forms, museum-dated 1898–99, signed "Louis C. Tiffany" and "L. C. T. D1414," 4½ in. high. Orange lava vase, speckled with white, museum-dated 1900, signed "L. C. Tiffany" in white paint,

numbered "D 1903," 5 in. high. Victoria and Albert Museum, London

BELOW RIGHT: Smoky green iris vase with brown floral motifs and dark green leaves, unsigned, with sticker "TGD Co." (Monogram), and "+2946" scratched on base, 12⅞ in. high. Price tag label $50.00, purchased at Tiffany and Company, Regent Street, 1896. Victoria and Albert Museum, London

58

ABOVE: Green and black vase with waves and swirls in tones of green, black and deep red in shallow relief, label and number "194" scratched on base, 7 in. high. Formerly, Coats-Connelly Collection

BELOW: Faceted agate vase in pale green and ochre, inscribed "L. C. Tiffany—Favrile c524," 11 in. high. Courtesy Lillian Nassau, New York

ABOVE: Paperweight vase (four layers) with flowing turbulent lava design on clear and sea-water background, inscribed "T 5133," 5 in. high. Courtesy Lillian Nassau, New York

BELOW: Vase, opaque ivory-colored background, with flowing blue and gold iridescent design, inscribed "L. C. T. L372," 5¼ in. high. Courtesy Lillian Nassau, New York

OPPOSITE: Green-gold iridescent Favrile vase with violet, green and blue swirls in slight relief, ca. 1900, Tiffany Glass and Decorating Company, inscribed "04536 Louis C. Tiffany," 10½ in. high. Collection, The Museum of Modern Art, New York. Phyllis B. Lambert Fund.

LEFT: Clear gold and iridescent glass vase with raised geometric pulled glass design, inscribed "L. C. Tiffany—Favrile 3660P," 5¾ in. high. Courtesy Lillian Nassau, New York

RIGHT: Blue iridescent vase with overall swirling pattern, inscribed "L. C. T. R 1279," 7 in. high. Courtesy Lillian Nassau, New York

some showpieces Favrile bowls displayed all their descriptive virtuosity and several even had "goldfish" floating amid "seaweed" in crystal clear "water."

Tiffany's earlier experimental forms were based closely on the most classic Roman shapes and on Islamic and Near Eastern glass. Gold pieces which were approximations of Roman vases were often given the corroded surface of buried glass and sometimes it was difficult to tell them from original Roman vases. The gold luster was produced either by direct application or by exposing it to vapors or gases in specially constructed furnaces; gold chloride could either be sprayed on, giving the vase a satiny texture, or suspended in the glass before it cooled, after which it would come to the surface. Twenty-dollar gold pieces were used as the base. Gold was also said to have been used to obtain the color of the much sought after red pieces.

In his book, Robert Koch claims that almost the entire glass-blowing production of 1894 was reportedly shipped to various museums, including the Smithsonian Institution (38 pieces), the Musée des Arts Décoratifs (50), the Imperial Museum of Fine Arts, Tokyo (23), and the Metroplitan Museum of Art, New York, presented by its first collector, Henry O. Havemeyer (56 pieces). By early 1896, with Bing's shop in full swing, Favrile was already on the general market in America and sold at Tiffany's studios or at his father's shops in New York and in London. Bing was its sole distributor on the Continent, and later organized an exhibition of the glass at the Grafton Galleries in London along with Tiffany windows designed by Frank Brangwyn. The Victoria and Albert Museum, London, bought many of its pieces from Tiffany and Company on Regent Street in 1896.

Generally speaking the variety of Tiffany Favrile glass is as follows: agate ware, paperweight pieces, iridescent vases, peacock vases, the flower-forms, marbled bottle vases, Roman corroded pieces, lava vases, the swan-neck vases (copies of Persian rose-water sprinklers) and laminated vases. Vasa Murrhina and cracklelure was also produced, along with pimple-surfaced "Nacreous" ware and "Cypriot" glass. Some of these could fit into the category of Accidentals whereby certain accidents of firing, blowing, or throwing produced abstract shapes and forms or misshapen characteristics which were admired for themselves. Some vases were cut and ground, and some etched, but on the whole the glass itself and what was inside it made up the major qualities of Favrile.

The art-for-art's-sake aesthetic that these vases symbolized was shrewdly summed up by an English critic Horace Townsend in the *Studio* of 1899 when Favrile glass was on show at the Grafton Galleries. Referring to the Accidentals, Townsend noticed that the spontaneous, immediate action of expressing line, color, and form in the material itself represented the true genius of Tiffany. For him the most intriguing works on show were the colored windows which allowed "accident to play even a larger part in the design" and where "figures, for instance, were represented entirely by the accidental effects produced by the manufacture of glass itself rather than by lines or shadows painted on a sheet of clear and evenly colored glass." Townsend preferred the vases in which "the decorative effects were obviously and frankly induced by aid of the ductility of the material alone." It is interesting to see at the turn of the century a taste developing for the act of creating itself, out of which the form grew without attention to pictorial content.

Cecilia Waern in the *Studio* a year or so earlier had seen the essential simplicity in Favrile despite its abstract quality:

Instances of contortion or intricacy are rare; the shapes are often capricious but with all the sweet waywardness of this exquisite material; they are almost invariably simpler, less slight, less tortured and more classical in the deepest sense, than the blown glass of Europe. They may recall shapes of Persia, Japan, Greece, because they have been *born* in the same way.

And it may not be too farfetched to see in Tiffany's Favrile glass the seeds of American abstract-expressionist painting which was to become so fashionable half a century later, about the same time that Tiffany glass underwent a revival of interest.

That Tiffany's vases brought to mind traditional pieces from Persia and other places is understandable if one visits the great collection of glass at the Victoria and Albert Museum which both Tiffany and Nash must have known well. Roman and Egyptian shapes are repeated by Tiffany as well as Persian glass from the 10th to the 17th century, many of the pieces colored by burial with a bright blue-gold iridescence. Other pieces at the museum would seem to have inspired Tiffany: 18th century English Nailsea glass with swirling striped decoration, marbled Venetian flasks of the 16th and 17th centuries called *calcedonio*, and some Bohemian pieces from the Blottendorf Factory (ca. 1830) which are prototypes of Tiffany's marbled agate-ware.

The dating of Tiffany Favrile has presented a problem since it was regularly and continuously produced until the Tiffany Furnaces were closed in 1928.

ABOVE: Gold iridescent vase, ca. 1900, inscribed "6159D L. C. Tiffany— Favrile," 6 in. high. Collection, The Museum of Modern Art. Purchase

BELOW: Blue-back vase, with gold iridescent spiral, ca. 1903, inscribed "L. C. Tiffany—Favrile 2326c," 6 in. high (sight). Courtesy Lillian Nassau, New York

ABOVE: Gold iridescent Favrile vase, inscribed "7873B L. C. Tiffany—Favrile," 10¾ in. high. Collection, The Museum of Modern Art, New York. Gift of Joseph H. Heil

BELOW: Group of iridescent vases in classical style, gold tinged with blue, vase on extreme left unlabeled, inscribed (left to right): "5011E," "5012E," "52E," "9916C," 6⅛ in., 6½ in., 10⅜ in., 6⅛ in. high. Haworth Art Gallery, Accrington, England. Gift of the family of Charles Briggs

(Tiffany Studios, a name which was incorporated in 1900, continued in business selling off old stock until it declared itself bankrupt in 1932.) The invention and originality went out of Favrile when Arthur Nash retired in 1919 and his sons took over; the production was cut down and only the most ordinary pieces were produced. But while Nash, senior, was running the Tiffany Furnaces, established in 1902, many early pieces were repeated if they proved to be popular, and from around 1900 to 1919 there is no traceable stylistic development in the glass to indicate date.

The one clue to dating lies somewhere in the elaborate and still-to-be-deciphered system of numbering on the glass itself. Since no known records exist, any numbering system offered is a matter for speculation. Robert Koch, without citing his sources, advances a system which he claims when coordinated with a change in the wording of labels affixed to objects (effected in 1900), "makes it possible to date most unusual examples with a fair degree of accuracy. Those which have prefixes from A to N were produced from 1896 to 1900, those with a prefix from P to Z from 1901 to 1905, those with a suffix from A to N from 1906 to 1912, those with a suffix from P to Z from 1913 to 1920." However, this presupposes that when Tiffany and Nash began numbering, they *knew* their direct control of the output of the glass would more or less end around 1920 at the exact moment when the alphabetical lettering reached Z, an assumption somewhat difficult to accept. Mr. Koch says that "the prefix X meant Not for Sale" (doesn't that become confused with the prefix X that indicates the year?) and that "the prefix O, which indicated special orders . . . was assigned to some exceptional pieces." (This seems more reasonable since the O in this case is of a different size than the numbers that follow.)

The earliest pieces were not signed, but Mr. Koch maintains that those that were given numbers bear the prefix X (presumably also meaning "not for sale"?) and that "later pieces not meant for sale were also marked with an X engraved near the base." Paper labels were stuck to the bottom of the first vases for sale, and examples survive containing two paper labels—one with a registry number and the other with a monogram indicating either the Tiffany Glass and Decorating Company (a large T with the D and the G at the terminal points of the hood of the T, with Co. at the base) or, much rarer, the Tiffany Glass Company (a large T with the G tucked under the left and the C tucked under the right of the hood of the T, the entire monogram in a circle). There is at least one example, in the Metropolitan Museum, of a vase with an extremely rare early label which says "Tiffany Fabrile Glass" and gives the stock number 9. This marbled bottle vase is dated about 1893–94.

As Mr. Koch rightly points out, "labels are quite perishable and some pieces of Tiffany blown glass made as early as 1894 or 1895 exist but no longer bear any identifying marks. These, however, are quite rare and of a quality that is readily recognizable."

The only reference to the numbering system made by Tiffany himself that is known appears in a letter of 1926 in which he says: "Each article of Favrile glass is marked with the Tiffany name or initials, and all unusual pieces bear a number, the letters of the alphabet being used first as a prefix, later as a suffix to the numbers." Does this indicate that pieces thought not to be unusual had no numbers or letters? And yet, some of the most unusual pieces (in our eyes) have neither. Tiffany's name was signed in one of several ways: either "L. C. Tiffany" or "Louis C. Tiffany" in a cursive hand, or a more rectilinear signature that ranged from "L. C. T." to "L. C. Tiffany-Favrile." Arthur Nash was the only other person allowed to sign pieces with the inscription "Sample—approved by A. J. Nash." The most prized pieces are ones that are marked "A-Coll." Known as "A-Collection pieces," these were meant for Tiffany himself, and yet several such pieces found their way into museums at an early date. Other curious pieces have round holes blown in the bottom, supposedly to indicate that they were stock models for the showroom and not meant to be sold. No other explanation is feasible, unless of course such pieces were trial exercises in the endless experimentation with form and color and texture that went on at the Tiffany furnaces.

Another method of dating has been offered by Stuart P. Feld of the Metropolitan Museum, in an article in the Metropolitan Museum of Art *Bulletin*. Mr. Feld, who had the advantage of studying some of the earliest pieces available with accurate dating of accession from the careful records kept of the Havemeyer Bequest, disagrees that the numbers refer to the date of order of production of the objects. His reasons are in the evidence contained in the Tiffany inventory. He says:

A piece dated 1903, for instance, is numbered 113A, while another dated 1910 is inscribed 46A. On the other hand, these dateable pieces from Tiffany's collection do convincingly suggest a correlation between number and design. Four reproductions of antique glass, for example, all dating from 1912, bear

ABOVE: Favrile iridescent vase, gold tones on dark background, ca. 1900, inscribed "09909," 9¼ in. high. Hessisches Landesmuseum, Darmstadt

BELOW: Agate vase, shading from yellow to pale green to black-green, signed with label, inscribed "5025E," 7½ in. high. Haworth Art Gallery, Accrington, England. Gift of the family of Charles Briggs

OPPOSITE: Millefiore paperweight vase (9 layers) with blossoms and swirling design in green, ochre, yellow and white, inscribed "R2401 Louis C. Tiffany," 8⅛ in. high. Exhibited at the Turin Exhibition in 1902. Collection, President Hugh F. McKean, Rollins College, Winter Park, Florida

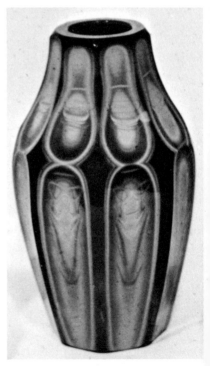

the numbers 7238J, 7239J, 7247J, and 8319J; another vase, also simulating ancient glass, falls into the same numerical sequence with the number 7252J, despite the fact that it is dated four years earlier. Two paperweight bowls . . . inscribed R2413 and R2415, appear to be part of the same sequence as a related bowl . . . inscribed R2420, in the Joseph Heil Collection at the Museum of Modern Art: a number of similar instances might be cited.

So might a number of dissimilar ones: for instance, a paperweight vase in the Coats-Connelly Collection similar in style to the two above-mentioned with a blown aperture at the base is inscribed "L.C.T. Y5617" (there is around two and a half inches difference in height among all three). Just to add to the confusion, vases with blown apertures in their base seem always to be favored with a Y prefix. Moreover, the swan-necked vase in the Coats-Connelly Collection is numbered M4374 while one like it at the Victoria and Albert Museum, London, is numbered +1279.

And here is another mark that is not accounted for: the curious + sign that is prefixed before two pieces in the Victoria and Albert. Did this indicate pieces for sale in London? If so, why do other pieces bought at the Regent Street shop not have the + sign? One piece, the swan-necked vase or Persian perfume-sprinkler marked +1279 is dated 1896 in the inventory (512-1896, price £3. 14. 3d.). The other, a green iridescent vase with "broad leaves alternating with pod-bearing stems in green and brown," is marked +2946 and has the label of Tiffany Glass and Decorating Company, and a price tag of $50.00. It also was bought at the Regent Street shop and is dated 1896 in the inventory (514-1896, price £10. 6. 2d.). There is no stylistic similarity, no size similarity, no color similarity, and their prices vary.

It is clear that until every number of every known Tiffany vase is correlated to every known date of museum acquisition and accurate stylistic comparisons are made, the numbering system will remain a tantalizing quasi mystery, always within grasp of deciphering, and yet always presenting some exception to wreck yet another hypothesis.

Apart from the red pieces, the most sought after Favrile are the paperweight vases. Technically they present the most complicated glassmaking problems and contain the most difficult feats of execution with overlays of glass, involved patternings, and complex figurations inside the glass. Modern glassmakers today still claim they cannot tell how they were done. The agate pieces, with their sides faceted or cut with vertical panels, the variegated colors complementing the faceting, are also highly prized, as are the lava pieces with their roughened, textured, and pitted surfaces resembling chunks of cooled lava, sometimes with stones or pebbles set into the glass. The flower forms, at one time thought too fragile to be popular among collectors, have come into their own and their importance both to Tiffany and to the development of Continental Art Nouveau cannot be underestimated. The Accidentals have proved the most fashionable, since they predict trends in mid-twentieth century abstract painting. Indeed, they are remarkable for their freeness of form which, despite the casual appearance, always bears a close relationship to the intricate color rhythms caught within the glass. The vagaries of changing taste being what they are, we might still witness a return to favor of the simple classical vases, based on Roman or Persian prototypes, which are as timeless as they are perfect.

From the moment Tiffany's fame was established in Europe, a bewildering variety of imitators followed suit. The most important one was the factory of Johannes Loetz Witwe of Klostermuhl, in Austria. Under the directorship of Max Ritter von Spaun, who designed most of the glass, Loetz Witwe never quite equaled Tiffany, although it closely followed examples which filtered through to Austria and Germany from France as early as the time of the founding of the first Vienna Secession in 1897. The silky texture so prized in Tiffany eluded Loetz Witwe, probably because the Austrian company was attempting to produce an iridescent glass along more economical lines. Still, some earlier examples of such glass are the closest thing to Tiffany that was produced, and not a few examples have been sold in the past as early unsigned pieces of Tiffany, or, more strangely, as early examples of Arthur Nash before he went to America! That Loetz Witwe was reaching for an international market is evidenced by the fact that some pieces around 1900 are signed "Loetz Austria," and marked with a crossed arrow device in a circle. This also spikes the belief that the Viennese firm was consciously attempting to fool the public into thinking the glass was by Tiffany. Less adventurous with forms, Loetz Witwe achieved some remarkable iridescent effects in both gold and in blue-green, green-blue-yellow, and brown-blue-green, but the range of color experimentation was narrow and the iridescence had a more metallic surface luster than Tiffany's. Of the other "copiers" of Tiffany in Europe, none of them come close to Loetz Witwe except Harrach, who made some convincing pieces in the manner of Tiffany. Karl Koepping,

LEFT: Flower-form vase, green striations on clear glass reaching upward in a leaf pattern tinged with bright red and covering a smoky white bulb-shaped blossom, inscribed "02508," 10 in. high. Private Collection, London

OPPOSITE: One of a pair of antique *verde* finish bronze candlesticks, with iridescent blue-pink glass balls blown and inset into the metal, ca. 1900, 18 in. high. Private Collection, London

RIGHT: Flower-form Favrile vase with silvered bronze base and top of glass, striated in green and white rising to a white flower whose interior is orange iridescent bordered in pale yellow, ca. 1900, inscribed "Tiffany Studios New York CL CO 1795 25695 101604," (?), 15⅞ in. high. Collection, The Museum of Modern Art, New York. Phyllis B. Lambert Fund

who is considered an imitator by some, is much maligned. Even if he had obliquely been inspired by Tiffany flower forms, Koepping's stemware pieces, which are virtuoso feats of glassblowing, strive more for realistic effects in their shapes; some even have twisted stems and independent leaves sprouting from the base of the glass, while the cup of the glass remains totally conventional. These pieces, many as early as 1895–96, are a far cry from Tiffany's organically conceived, freely formed shapes. In any case, the tall etiolated stem form is not original to Tiffany or to Koepping. It existed in English glassware in the eighties and early nineties (William Powell and Sons created some beautiful specimens) and it was traditional in German glassware.

In America, around 1902, the Quezal Art Glass and Decorating Company of Brooklyn produced excellent opaque and iridescent glass shades in the manner of Tiffany. Victor Durand at the Vineland Flint Glassworks made clear glass vases and objects with delicate strands of green in the glass. But since both signed their glass, presumably they were attempting to satisfy a huge market at a cheaper price, rather than consciously creating forgeries. Later, pressed glass known as Carnival glass (because it was often the shooting-gallery prize at the local fair) which had a rather vulgar orangey-golden sprayed-on iridescence, became the cheapest—and the nastiest—debasement of Tiffany's product.

Robert Koch claims that "in terms of both quality and quantity" the glass most like Tiffany's was produced by Frederick Carder for Steuben. With the trade name of *Aurene*, the Steuben iridescent glass which Carder had perfected in England before coming to America and establishing his glassworks at Corning, New York, was a metallic glass with iridescent tones of gold or blue alternating with deep colors in ordinary glass. The shapes were identical to Tiffany's, who issued a lawsuit against Steuben in 1913. It was settled out of court since it was obvious that Tiffany did not invent iridescence, even if his pieces were the best examples.

In a study of Tiffany glass, one can only touch briefly on the other products that surged into the market from Tiffany Studios after it was founded in 1900. These included jewelry, enamelware, objects in a mixture of precious metals, and inlay pieces. Nash bought huge stamping presses which were capable of turning out a large amount of metalwork objects: cigarette boxes, desk sets, vanity sets for dressing tables, picture frames, cigar lighters, tobacco jars, jardinieres, clocks, and even twine-holders; all became known as "Wedding

Present Tiffany" since they had a certain chic, were not outrageously expensive, and were decorative as well as useful. After 1905, Tiffany began producing pottery objects in large numbers as well as in a variety of shapes, with a great range of glazes from rough to smooth. Any decoration was fired in the pot and not applied to the surface and each one was said to be unique. Naturally, they all had the familiar "L.C.T." on the bottom.

It is remarkable that with over a hundred craftsmen producing objects and glass, the Tiffany Studios and Tiffany Furnaces could still maintain their high level of originality and novelty without gimmickry. In this sense, Tiffany had found a solution of how to work within the terms of the "machine age" and still produce handcrafted articles. Here he followed the example set by Liberty of London who had also used metal presses to stamp out objects in pewter or silver plate, which were hand-finished with a variety of ornamental decorations to make each piece distinct.

The problem was to satisfy both the critic and the customer with an object produced by handicraft and at the same time permit the manufacturer to make the best use of the most modern machinery. Thus, the followers of William Morris proved that mass production need not necessarily diminish either craft or quality by taking advantage of lower costs to make wider distribution possible. But then, like Liberty, Tiffany could claim to have transformed the assembly line operation into a craft of its own with highly skilled glass workers deftly forming, shaping, throwing, blowing or rolling the glass under his, or Nash's direct supervision. Early examples of Tiffany were certainly handcrafted articles in the fullest sense of the word. But as the glass grew in popularity, and particularly when the glass shades began to be made in huge quantities, Tiffany Studios became a unique factory in which craftsmanship was successfully combined with assembly line production, partly aided by machinery. There is no other explanation for such an enormous output of glass which at the same time retained a remarkably high level of quality and variety. (Cecilia Waern noted in her visit to the studios, "5,000 colors and varieties are kept accessible" in the stockrooms.) In France, Gallé set up mass production, and after 1900 his glass began to appear stereotyped and the results were mechanical looking, something that never happened with Tiffany.

With the glass production Tiffany acted as *metteur en scène*; as the Diaghilev of Favrile he directed the craftsmen, made suggestions, offered solutions to problems, and kept tight control (with Arthur Nash) on everything that left the studio. All pieces had to bear the inimitable imprint of Tiffany Favrile. However, one gathers a great deal of freedom was given to the individual glassblowers and craftsmen after Tiffany or Nash had provided a rough color sketch of what they wanted. Tiffany's biographer, Charles de Kay, noted that "Mr. Tiffany cannot turn his sketch over to the foreman and expect results worthy of his reputation. He has to superintend every stage of the work just as carefully with the same zeal as during the evolution of an oil painting." Yet, the enormous output of Tiffany glass after 1900 would have made direct superintendence a physical impossibility and his role must have been that of artistic director.

The commercial aspect of Tiffany Studios, for which its founder was incessantly attacked by his competitors, reached its height with Tiffany lamps. Here he proved that both mass production and his much sought for "beauty" could go hand in hand, in the creation of objects which were intrinsically functional—if not essential. Moreover, it was here that his feeling for sculptural form found perfect expression in the bronze that was molded to hold or support the colored glass shades. Tiffany's experiments with light began quite early when he worked with Thomas Alva Edison on the Lyceum Theatre in 1885, designing chandeliers for the new incandescent lamp which was not patented until two years later. The Havemeyer residence had chandeliers of electric lights, but this was in advance of its time; meanwhile he worked with gas chandeliers and sconces and later with petroleum or kerosene. Around 1895, his petroleum lamps were on the market and, like the vases, they had a bulbous base of Favrile glass and a shade of opalescent, iridescent, or mother-of-pearl glass. The bases were marked with the monogram of the Tiffany Glass and Decorating Company. By 1897, Tiffany was using bronze forms as bases to support shades of leaded iridescent and colored glass for table or standing lamps, and an avant-garde German magazine *Deutsch Kunst und Dekoration* illustrated his petroleum lamps as the "latest thing" in 1900–1. Tiffany bronze lamps with the new marking "Tiffany Studios New York" were exhibited at the Paris Exhibition in 1900; these included the Dragonfly lamp (designed by Clara Driscoll) and the Dandelion lamp.

With the growing popularity of electricity (Edison's early light bulbs were blown at the Corning Glassworks) Tiffany put his mind to a series of lamps either with one shade covering a number of small bulbs or a number of small

ABOVE: Turtle-back lamp, bronze with green-blue iridescent glass, signs of zodiac on base, ca. 1900, 14 in. high. Collection, Mr. Charles Jerdein, London

BELOW: LEFT TO RIGHT: Brownish-green Favrile vase with overlay of glass in feather design, inscribed "L. C. Tiffany Favrile 6024K," 5½ in. high. Cypriot cream vase with violet and green flowers and leaves, and brown vines, inscribed "L. C. T. Louis C. Tiffany D127," 10½ in. high. Cypriot blue-black vase, with iridescent vines and leaves, signed "L. C. Tiffany Favrile 72443," 3½ in. high. Courtesy Lillian Nassau, New York

OPPOSITE: Bronze floor lamp with iridescent gold glass shades and lily-pad base, ca. 1900, unmarked, 55½ in. high. Called Lily-cluster lamp. Collection, The Museum of Modern Art, New York. Gift of Joseph H. Heil

BELOW LEFT: Table lamp in bronze and colored Favrile glass, ca. 1900, 27 in. high. It was designed by Mrs. Curtis Freshel and was one of the most popular lamps of the Tiffany Studios. Called the Wisteria lamp. Courtesy Lillian Nassau, New York

BELOW RIGHT: Table lamp in bronze and colored Favrile glass, lily-pad base, ca. 1900, plaque on shade inscribed "Tiffany Studios/New York," 26½ in. high. Called Lotus lamp. Courtesy Lillian Nassau, New York

bulbs each with an independent shade. That Tiffany, with his firsthand knowledge of the new invention and his understanding of the properties of transmitted and reflected light, should make lamps on a mass-production "handcrafted" basis, was a foregone conclusion. He aimed at designing shades which would screen the harsh light of the incandescent lamp and hide its ugly shape at the same time; his solution was an assortment of iridescent colors and wonderfully imaginative leaded glass designs, whose surfaces of rich blues, deep olives, and bright reds mingled with bronze-gold, would dazzle by day and when lit at night could turn into the brightest yellow, golden orange, and white, striped with purple and emerald green. When the Tungsten lamp appeared in 1903, its too-bright light needed the same treatment and Tiffany's solution was accepted as the most aesthetic and the most practical.

Bronze, which he had already used for candlesticks and other household objects, was worked into a number of highly sculptural forms, and the Tiffany lamp base became a work of art in its own right; lily pads, spider's webs, vine stems and tendrils, tree trunks, or shapes which bore no relationship to anything recognizable were incorporated. Openwork bronze was sometimes inset with iridescent balls of green glass blown inside the bronze openwork as a filler. In some instances, early Byzantine models were readapted with rope-beading and circular or zigzag motifs traced in relief over the bronze. The metal was usually finished in an antiqued green-brown color, its dark burnished surface contrasting dramatically with the glistening jewel-like glass. Many of the lamps had fitted shades, which were interchangeable, as well as moveable fixtures, and armatures so that light could be directly focused. Some models, such as the Wisteria lamp, were made in graded sizes. Taken as a whole the electric lamps seem to have been Tiffany's most satisfactory objects both from a plastic and utilitarian point of view, and it is hardly surprising that they have found a place in today's ultrafunctional interiors.

In 1902, Tiffany's Lily-cluster lamp, perhaps one of his most successful models along with the Wisteria lamp, won a prize at the Turin Exhibition. Composed of anywhere from three to twenty gold iridescent lily-shaped shades on long bronze stalks sprouting from a base of lily-pad leaves, it was one of his most original designs. The Wisteria lamp, designed in 1904 by Mrs. Curtis Freschel, as were many other lamps, had a huge umbrella-like shade of intricate leading made to look like the leaves and flowers of a hanging wisteria tree; with this lamp as with so many others, the experience and craftsmanship that had gone into Tiffany colored glass windows was readapted for more practical purposes. Other lamps had leaded glass flower patterns such as the daisy, the rose, the pansy, and the daffodil. Among more unusual varieties were snail-shaped shades and those which incorporated great rough hunks of glass known as turtleback. Among the most delicate were those that used a lacy motif, either resembling a spider's web or a piece of "Queen Anne" lace.

After his father's death in 1902, Tiffany concentrated on designing jewelry and enamels for the firm, rather than on new glass techniques. Another Englishman, Joseph Briggs, who was born at Accrington, Lancashire, and who had been with Tiffany since 1890, later became supervisor of his business affairs so that the direct responsibility for the Studios could be taken off his shoulders. It was the Briggs family who left to the Haworth Art Gallery their fine collection of Tiffany glass, comprising 73 Favrile vases, 7 mosaic pictures, 43 glass tiles and other objects, which is one of the finest single collections of Tiffany in Europe.

From 1902–4 he busied himself building a fantastic home at Oyster Bay, Long Island, called Laurelton Hall, which combined some of the purest elements of Art Nouveau with a mixture of Moorish, Byzantine, and oriental decor. It contained over eighty rooms and was said to have cost more than $2,000,000. It was destroyed by fire in 1957. Photographs of the main hall and the dining room indicate a prevailing pattern of large clear surfaces, structural emphasis, and simplified form despite a rampant eclecticism. Light-colored furniture, Eastern fabrics, stenciled wall decorations, brightly colored decorative tiles, and the inevitable hanging glass lamps were employed with restraint and dignity, lending an air of implied rather than stated lavishness.

In this exotic yet spiritually contemporary setting, Tiffany gave three pageants that astounded even New York society, which was accustomed to such events. The first was an Egyptian fête, for which he transformed the entire end of his studio into a representation of the Nile. Guests were invited to mingle with "Egyptian beauties, bare-legged youths and Pinkerton men (private detectives) in oriental guise." With Europe on the threshold of war, he invited 150 gentlemen in 1914 to "inspect the spring flowers"—a stag occasion in which young ladies in classical draperies carried live peacocks on their shoulders in a procession around the dining table; peacock was the main course. On his birthday in 1916, he gave a breakfast for over two hundred which was enlivened by a masque called "The Quest for Beauty," played by

LEFT: Table lamp in verdigris bronze and amber tinted Favrile glass, base in shape of upturned mushroom, shade in form of spider web, ca. 1900, marked "Tiffany Studios, New York '(7)337," 18 in. high. Called Spider lamp. Collection, The Museum of Modern Art, New York. Phyllis B. Lambert Fund

OPPOSITE: Hanging Dragonfly lamp in Favrile glass, ca. 1900. A variation of the lamp designed by Clara Driscoll, which won a prize in Paris in 1900. Courtesy Lillian Nassau, New York

forty-five actors and described as an "exceptionally artistic dramatization of the history of art, the story of the impulses which eventually found expression in the skill of the human hands."

Although he saw himself as the American William Morris, and in many ways as a more sophisticated answer to Liberty of London, Tiffany proved to be a poor vehicle for the later English Arts and Crafts movements, which hoped to bring a better standard of everyday practical design to the growing middle classes. But even Cecilia Waern, steeped as she was in the ideals of her compatriots, had to admit that in America, where the taste for Tiffany reigned supreme, "it would be almost absurd to expect a serious 'return to simplicity' in the land of mushroom fortunes (and) social strugglers. . . ."

Where Tiffany succeeded was in opening up avenues of aesthetic invention to his countrymen which were not based on previous European-inspired models, but rather on nature's organic forms which owed their invention to nothing but themselves. It is this non-objective, abstract quality which perhaps helped the generation of the early 1950's to see the intrinsic merit in both Tiffany glass and Art Nouveau as it related to the avant-garde painting of

the time. In fact, Favrile glass appeared as an uncanny precedent to Abstract Expressionism; and when America's first great international contribution to contemporary painting was hardening into a movement in the early fifties, Tiffany glass—which itself depended so much on the principles of controlled accident, color, shape, and free-form design—found new admirers.

As Edgar Kaufmann, jr., analyzed it in an influential article in *Interiors* magazine in 1955, the relevance of Tiffany to contemporary taste was that of "accident" and that "this love of controlled accident is one of Tiffany's strong links to the modern design of our day; for modern artists and designers have paralleled theoretical physicists in their fascination with the random chances that underlie dependable appearances."

Tiffany's reputation today rests on something more solid than the vagaries of fashionable ornament or stylistic revivals, for he has rightly been credited with being one of America's greatest designers who reshaped one of the world's oldest crafts into a new, lapidary form of art.

Iridescent plate with peacock feather design, ca. 1900, inscribed "L. C. T. κ2423,"
6¼ in. diameter. Courtesy Lillian Nassau, New York